CHECK

Check

SARAH TOLMIE

McGill-Queen's University Press

Montreal & Kingston • London • Chicago

ISBN 978-0-2280-0363-2 (paper)
ISBN 978-0-2280-0521-6 (ePDF)
ISBN 978-0-2280-0522-3 (ePUB)

Legal deposit fourth quarter 2020
Bibliothèque nationale du Québec

Printed in Canada on acid-free paper that is 100% ancient forest free
(100% post-consumer recycled), processed chlorine free

We acknowledge the support of the Canada Council for the Arts.

Nous remercions le Conseil des arts du Canada de son soutien.

Library and Archives Canada Cataloguing in Publication

Title: Check/Sarah Tolmie.

Names: Tolmie, Sarah, author.

Series: Hugh MacLennan poetry series.

Description: Series statement: The Hugh MacLennan poetry series |
Poems.

Identifiers: Canadiana (print) 20200340239 | Canadiana (ebook)
2020034028X | ISBN 9780228003632 (softcover) |
ISBN 9780228005216 (PDF) | ISBN 9780228005223 (ePUB)

Classification: LCC PS8639.O45 C54 2020 | DDC C811/.6—dc23

This book was typeset by Marquis Interscript in 9.5/13 Sabon.

With thanks to Madhur, Tanis, Laurie, and Pam

We almost always excuse that which we understand.
Mikhail Lermontov, *A Hero for Our Time*

I am right about everything.

☐

Other people are sadly wrong.

☐

Many people agree with me.

☐

Crazy people must be kept at bay.

☐

But I concede –

☐

☐

☐

☐

☐

The world is one big leading question.
Slick chutes and boxes made of teflon.

Tick boxes, gun sights, Instagram accounts,
shunt all the people where we want
them to be:

following, or far away

My teenage daughter just asked me:
What's a self-fulfilling prophecy?
Oh, it's when an utterance makes things true,
I said, as if I said to you: you're going to die
On Tuesday, and in anxiety, you do.
Ah, she said, and ticked a mental box
And went away to herd her teenage flocks.

Later I thought I should have said much more.
These things go right down to the core.
If you think, it's not my fault, I am betrayed,
The world betrays me, you will find
People do it every time.
If in your heart you blame the women or the Jews
You will see indictment in the news.
Such prophecies make you a Liberal or a Tory.
They forecast the end of every story.
So great is their power that they are
Indistinguishable from laws.
Expect the ball to fall, it falls.

We have proleptic evidence
We knew already how it went.
I knew you'd ask me this, I should have said.
I am the mother, you the daughter.
I know exactly how this ends.

Hairless apes, while they're alive
Need a community to thrive.
Bald fact.

Do you remember that old saw:
All recognize the beautiful
As beautiful, and therein lies –

Ugliness?
There's that.

Let us compare our terrible scars.
Mine is deeper than yours by far.

Can we put the rape back into the lock
By shaming the prisoner in the dock?

It's improper to objectivize.
So we blindfold all our eyes
And pin the tails on, asinine.

God and all his marching men forbid and forbid again.
Why do people listen to them?
They agree to disagree.
Consent's an oil-rich currency.
It's keto, paleo, gluten-free
And gives us friends.

Here's a list of words we do not use.
Inclusively, we don't include
Anyone who uses them.

Culture is war. Everything that's said
Is disagreed with, A to Z.
What then do you ask of me?

Political correctness is a thing
Like eczema or marketing.

It isn't human decency,
The wish for change or equity –
These have their names –
It is that strange
Moment when authority
Denies itself.

When people with power, platform, wealth,
Pretend that they're somebody else.
When status speaks like a gilded slave
Pleading from well-appointed cage

And we're expected to believe
Complacent faces, pale, aggrieved,
Who tell us how we should behave
Because they're attuned to others' needs.

What happens to compassion then?
Towards the women by the men?
Towards the brownish by the pink?
Consider what most people think!

Betterment is slow. You want it fast.
Rarely is this power in your grasp.
So others act on your behalf.

This is a two-edged sword.
But then, it's an imperfect world.

For most people, most things suck.
Sometimes they're decent on the bus,
That think tank of the populace.

People grumble, hedge, ignore
Glare and make small signs of war
But from time to time they pat the seat
And invite you to get off your feet.

In my opinion we all do well
In such situations not to kill ourselves.
Gold stars all round.
Plus, in Canada, we're not armed.

We're on the bus, getting through the day.
We really don't want our consciousness raised.

Professors worry about intersections
because they all drive.

At a Kitchener greasy spoon:

"Did you hear all that about the Toronto Board?
Yeah, they've just gone and banned the word
Chief. Chief, like in CEO.
On the doors, the letterhead, it all has to go.
It's insulting to natives, so they say.
D'ya think they consulted the community?
D'ya think one single chief was asked?
What would native leaders think about that?
What a wonderful use of public money!
It's hilarious, really, just so funny.
God knows schools got no other worries."

It takes the Hippocratic oath to save an educator.
Most people wouldn't pass them a defibrillator.

God knows our choices are sacrosanct.
Most lead directly to the bank.
We choose our friends; we choose our groups;
Our hookups, our husbands, our helpers, our hopes.
And our villains too. They come pre-loaded.
Pre-felt, prescribed, encoded.
In front of the guns in the first-person shooters
Or in any other places we might disapprove of.

Big data comforts our small minds.
It boosts the scale of our enterprise.
If something happens a million times
Then it's a trend and we are wise.

Heaven forfend that we should concentrate
On this or that outlying case,
On details that leave no trace
Except in art or what people say.

High numbers lead to higher truth.
We demonstrate our social worth
By thinking demographically
To prove what everyone can see.

We'd waste our time should we explain
Things unforeseen and small and strange.

There are certain words I've come to hate.
Pedagogy. Praxis. Innovate.
B-R-A-N-D-I-N-G is what they do to cattle.
Societal means no more than social.
Granular is a quality of sand.
Euphemism is driving me mad.
Digital means I give you the finger.
And *virtual* is the scent that lingers
In a room full of wannabes.

Mr Pope with his poison pen
Made a slam dunk now and again,
Slipping that ball right through the hole
Like a giant seven-foot tall.
Sometimes saying the obvious thing
Is perfectly satisfying.

If I stop my ears with wax
Maybe they'll take the headphones back.

Wax can be had, melt and pour,
From the aisle of the craft supply store:
Melt product completely. Allow to cool.
Insert into ears while still pliable.
Then, and only then, tie yourself to the mast.
A nice braided cotton or hemp will last.

Hang quiet and limp as the sirens scream:
Agree, agree, just agree. Agree.

Assent is a curious act.
You can't agree, for example, with a fact.
It does not admit of opinion.

Gravity exerts its dominion
Whether you say yea or nay.
You don't disagree and float away.

Evolution or misogyny
Do not care what you believe.
Nor your friends or commander-in-chief.

Often we're invited to discuss
Matters that just aren't up to us.

Might as well argue with a compass needle
As pretend global warming isn't due to people.

A fact isn't a question, request or reproof.
It really requires nothing from you.

I have to admit I'm a coterie poet.
Three dozen readers certainly know it.
Future biographers gamely will show it.
A modest award from the league will bestow it.

It's a coterie business, the poetry gig.
Audiences are small but some prizes are big.
Millions of people think we're irrelevant
But we keep going just for the hell of it.

Ah, the poets of Instagram.
The self-crowning laureates of our time.
You can't deny it worked for Napoleon.
Even the Lifestyle pages extol them.

Stupid old fart. Okay, boomer,
Deny the art of the media consumer.
I don't deny it. Look. There it is.
With celebrity diets and dick pics and tits.

On the crest of that wave, Instagram poets craft their own fame.
More people, more porn.
That's what media's for.
Poets have always jammed feet in that door.

I appreciate words in a big marketplace
But I don't need my poetry giving good face.

Praise comes too late
In traditional media.
So people tweet.

Say something wise,
Get paid on time.
Why should I wait

Until my wit is past its use-by date?
Three years ago I had this thought? Or five? Or ten?
Change up the dates in the MS again?
Smile like the actor on the promo tour
For the film he thinks he did, but can't be sure?

OMFG.
Tweet it and get the praise today.

Oscar Wilde made few mistakes in print
Or in his heart as he wrote for it.
His *bon mots* cost him all. He died of wit,
Thinking his fans his friends and taking risks
Allowed by vanity that was too well served
By salon minions hanging on his words.

If a mind as fine and sweet and sonorous as his
Was so destroyed, I will be quiet, as less pure.
I will stick to that one thing of which I'm sure:
Art in its slow making's joy.

Slow food's cuisine.
Slow sex is love.
Slow praise is what true art deserves.

Mr Auden said, on a particular day
Speaking in his universal way:
Law is like love.

Here is a tale of singular they.
Several laws were disobeyed.
Where love comes in I could not say.

An assistant in a first-year class
Showed an op-ed video that
Railed against non-binary

Pronouns
(a professor on TV
provided this, conveniently)

The professor called the assistant in.
He glared and said, what have you done?
You're paid to do what the syllabus says.

This is not a course in cultural studies
Where we examine old fuddy-duddies
And what they say in the media.

Law says you're teaching communication.
That's what they bought with their tuition.

Please consult your funding package.
Understand that embarrassing fracas
Can follow breaking of the law.

Say you depart so from your brief.
Students will come to me with grief
As the professor of the class –

We feel non-binary today
And where on the syllabus does it say
That we learn this, specifically?

A syllabus is a tool of law.
We feel this contract has a flaw.

The assistant then burst into tears.
How do we know? Well, it appears
She recorded all that was said.

This is against the law, but she
Felt that invasion of privacy
In this case was justified.

Women teaching have it rough.
It's only sense to be proactive.
We're all browbeaten quite enough.

She sent the file to a journalist
Who then used it to insist
That the assistant was victimized.

Free speech was compromised,
That law most sacred to reporters.
Lo, what kankedort is

The university president in?
Which of these laws should win?

The laws of traditional English grammar?
A teacher's right to think untrammelled?
That the syllabus should be honoured?
Non-binarists seen to be alive?
That civil servants should be bothered
To follow the forms that are prescribed?
That supervisors should supervise?
Women not be made to feel small?
Or students get what they're paying for?
What a nightmare is the law.

And then there is the law of blog
That always helps the underdog.
Blog helps those who help themselves.

Caught between these many laws
The president's solution was
Simply to apologize.

Apology to law's oblique.
Their edges don't quite meet.
But where law's despised and love forgotten
It's what we have, Mr Auden.

Despair is retrograde
But has its points
I have to say.

The flatline that you share with Lear
Means all signs of life are worth a cheer.
However small, they count as spikes.

Optimists are rarely nice.
Most are judgemental fucks
Who expect us all to have their luck.

Spirulina and a positive attitude
Will spare you being eaten by cannibals.

A daily antioxidant   .
Prevents the failure of your bank.

Illuminati will divulge
How to change those pesky bulbs.

The new Sermon on the Mount
Appeared in his Pinterest account.

Your life will be saved by an acronym
But you only remember how it begins.

Death metal. Ghost pepper. Total paralysis.
Here in the world of internet challenges.
You've shaved your head, done the ice cube tank.
Then your Fitbit says you should walk the plank.

The tech school president is an algorithm
Who proceeds from hot links given
Out in ordinary speech.
These he parses and seems to reach
An approximation of meaning
By context-sensitive strings and seeming
Groomed and receptive, like a sex doll.
He is president of Westworld.

If I shot this volume into space
Or into a mountain, metres deep
To be extracted in the race
For the next clean fuel technology
That would be something he'd need to see.
I'm nothing to him, nor him to me.
Engineers make things that we don't need
And poets write books that we don't read.

Why would anyone waste a single calorie
In the political shooting gallery?
Clay pigeons lined up to be shot
By whistleblowers, ready or not?

Do you really want to read the memoir
Of the Holocaust denier?
The builder of Humpty Dumpty's wall?
Who cares about these men at all?

Shut up, you privileged solipsist!
What, you think you're off the grid?

World tech expo 2018.
Innovation trumped by rain.

The technocratic ark
Sinking slowly in the dark.

Gadget makers, give us more!
If only we could find the door.

Some people read Greek
And some read Latin.
One of two things can happen.

Greek is some linear squiggles
About old misogynist homosexuals.
You're stuck holding a frameless door
To a world that isn't there anymore.

Greek is in your mind.
Greek is hard and rare.
So, if anyone cares, you who read
Are a timeless authority.

We haul noseless statues hither and yon
With no idea what went on
In the silence of the Parthenon.

Purity is yours
And vatic grace
And we have to believe
Everything you say.

Compared to that
Latin is half-assed.
We all know the letters: A B C.
They make up our reality.

Latin buildings and roads and laws
Surround us from the Rome that was.
Half of us still believe in their God.

Greek is vacation but Latin is home.
Europe shipped it clear round the globe.
Greek ships are long sunk with their fiery sails
Leaving nothing behind but a few billionaires.
The problem with Latin is everyone knows it.
It's kicking around just under our noses
Too familiar to see.
Folks may be charmed by our cute etymologies
But a lot of their basic psychology
Is Latin already.
That text is woven.
We can pluck and fret, readjust some old threads.
But basically, Latin ain't dead.

Matchy-matchy rhyme's okay.
Beats those nude shoes any day:
Poetry you don't know is there.

Fail faster
Fail better
In poetry's ugly sweater.

the pataphysical poet
is having a great time
and we all know it

that's how he wins
he thumbs his nose
as our lips grow thin

plugged or unplugged
or grown in a vat
there is just no
competing with that

old dada attitude
all criticism it converts to gratitude
cunning machine
that refuses to work
and never explains

Buried here beneath the slate
We've left it a little late
Over in Poets' Corner.

Mumph mumph mumble mumble
No-one hears a word we say.
Really, it's no wonder.

Six feet under the world is still.
There's time to read the manual
Of life, uninterrupted.

Feet dash and shuffle up above
Exhausted and corrupted.
Here down below we're snug and slow

Pondering old questions.
Custodians buff up our stones, addressing tourist messes,
While we, collections of rattling bones, lie here sly and quiet.

AR rats will try to raise us and put us on the tour,
With glasses and with goggles they will peer beneath the
    floor
And bid us rise, augmented, to entertain once more.

Dead poets read for free, they say, what does it really matter?
Underneath designer footwear we'll raise unholy clatter.

We're sexist racist ageist ableist; we will swear and scare
    your kids.
Leave us, tour operators. We would rather just be dead.

We will fold our barren fingers and purse our withered mouths
And go on thinking thoughts in the space that we're allowed.

Poetry is a convenience food:
Crunchy chips of thought that come pre-chewed
In little tear-off packages.

Vitaminized with sweet intelligence,
Packed with umami sentences
And technical deliciousness.

Therefore, it isn't good for you.
Afterwards you feel a fool:
Confused, and a little queasy.

Digesting poems isn't easy.
They're fat and salt and full of bones
Boiled down and wrapped in paper.

Dubious treats that you'd be better
Having just occasionally.
So all moral experts say.

They are the bouillon cubes of art:
Small and square and dark and hard
And no-one knows what they're made of.

Also, they are allergenic.
In many people they cause panic,
Swelling, and shortness of temper.

Shelf-stable, they will last forever,
Ichiban in crinkly covers.

An unsold book's like an ingrown hair.
Quarto pacemaker dug in there,
Stretching the skin of your chest,
Insisting it knows what's best.

A book that isn't in press
Is nowhere.

Agents, editors lag
As you pack your bag
And try to get away.
Baby's not born today.

This is writer's block.
Not what happens to every hack
Who claims he's got a novel in him,
The only problem is *beginning*.

Go, little book,
So that people can say that my first book was better
And reviewers discuss my *sophomore effort*
Though I wrote four books in the interim
That weren't novels.
Go, second, needy child
And be competitive and win all the prizes.
Pay back the taxpayers.
Rouse the agent from her ill-timed retirement.
Chiefly, little book
Just go.
Get out of my head.
Come back if there are film options,
And then, only long enough for me to sign.
Go, and let me forget the 11-day gap in my life like Agatha
    Christie's
In which I stared you down in a hotel room,
Sphinx without a secret. Empty bitch.
A week in a bikini really shows you what you've got.
Break, break, break.

Genre makes the problem plain.
The avant garde are such a pain.
It's the blind leading the blind.

We all swan dive off the cliff
Or stand in splendiferous
Silence in a swamp for eighteen years.
Genre mitigates our fears.

New things are best mixed in with old
Familiar patterns that our minds can hold.
Truth be told, new things are overrated.
Most of us cannot explain them.
This gives us anxiety.
We turn to the healing balm
Of ownership, or expertise.

A known genre lets things be.
Repeatability
Creates scientific truth.

Thrillers thrill, romances romance,
Avengers find their audience.
Only infant joy gets lost
With too much map, too little land.

Sales get rid of the stigma of genre.
Consider how well Margaret Atwood recovered
From SFF (that infectious disease).
Now she's a writer of speculative fiction.
Meanwhile the rest of us still have to listen
With our heads bowed
To Cormac McCarthy slog down the road
Through a Ruined Earth that's a century old.
McEwan writes of a robot named Adam
And critics with banners raised flock out to greet him
Armed with their Star Trek jokes
When what they've bought is a pig in a poke.
Overripe ham and pure blowing smoke.

It's always the next thing, isn't it?
This explains futurologists, otherwise inexplicable.
You've finished x and are working on y.
X is out in the world.
People call you up and ask what occurred
During its making. You can barely remember
And for sure do not care.
You gather your wits and attempt to share
Landmarks from a place you know you once were,
Like a drunk tourist.
No wonder people think authors are dumb
Compared to their books.
The books are done.
We, works in progress, are moving on.
It is best to treat writers as dead.
We've done what we've done and said what we've said.
Insofar as we are still alive, we want your cash and the
    occasional prize
To leverage the next thing. Reviews are bizarre.
It's like giving advice at a funeral.
Nothing we can do now.
Readers may need consumer advice
But all of our efforts are boxed up tight in those small sturdy
    coffins
You hold in your fists.
The gods themselves cannot recall their gifts.

Movies exist for destruction of cars.
Who can count how many there are
Smashed in one single chase?
Why even bother looking both ways?

A man stands with a whip or a shield or a handgun
And faces down the speeding dragon.
No-one gets through the intersection.

Driving is bad for your health.
On the highway's altar we destroy our wealth
Spectacularly in blood and fire.

How we hate our cars. Look how we fear them.
May they smash and burn for the sake of our children
Squashed in the drive, and for every victim of DUI.

Or maybe Mazda and Ford
Want us to smash them
So we buy more.

Cops die in the cars and bad guys are fried.
Soccer moms in vans, Latinos in hot rods,
Go up in flames, sacrificed to the road gods.

They stay behind. Heroes walk away
And we follow them and leave the debris.

Mortal Engines was a monstrous bomb.
Personally, I found nothing wrong, or nothing
Worse than usual.
The antipodes received it well
As everyone's relatives were in it.

Americans don't like steampunk.
Brokenhearted eurojunk can just stay home;
We want no *bricolage* today.
(All except for Neil Gaiman
Who somehow managed to persuade them
Canon fodder is okay.)

Bowie fixed his teeth to take New York.
Americans like things to work.

Someone compared me to Dorothy Parker.
And while this was thrilling, it made me think darkly:
I'm not American.
Who would be now?
It's just embarrassing.
But then, snarky feminists short on sobriety
Are not cherished by every society.

Alcoholism is a stackable pathology.
It fits over top of whatever insanity
You've got already.

What is addiction if not depression?
Compulsion, mania, obsession?
Bipolarity? Psychosis?

Drink's rarely a sole diagnosis.
Addiction is not the thing-in-itself.
It's a symptom you can treat.

Rehab gets people on their feet.
But if you take their booze away
Underneath they're still cray-cray.

A reformed drunk is a drunk not drinking
But there's no telling what she might be thinking.

I admit I have brewed kombucha.
All the other people who do so
Talk with the sourdough-starters online.

The low-carbers cut them dead
With their sugars and their bread.
Out of ketosis they'll never thrive.

There are people who never worry
With enough turmeric in their curry
For anti-inflammatory reasons.

In Canada the hundred-mile diet
Leaves you with cabbages if you try it
For two out of the four seasons.

And all of this is perfectly fine
As long as I can have it with wine.

Back in the 1980s
My friend joined the merchant navy.
As third mate he learned the ropes.
Like any pirate, he had hopes.
Then the Iron Lady tightened her belt
And the fleet went all to hell.
All the young were cast away
On a barren isle in the North Sea
While guys who had seniority
Rowed away, thanking their lucky stars.
He lit a signal fire. So did his friends.
But nobody ever came for them.

Years later, to cope with this adversity
He enrolled in university.
He smoked and fucked and studied his way
Through a literature degree.

I lost touch with him shortly after
He moved on to these greener pastures.
What he does now I don't know
But I'd like to think that thar he blows.

In the organic brain
Redundancy's a useful thing.
Neurons don't mind being fired.

It's very hard while you're alive
To realize you are obsolete.
That the flagship of your fleet

Was rechristened while you looked away
Through a telescope or were in the head.
Come back, your career is dead.

Your epaulettes begin to sag
As they hoist another flag.
There you are mid-ocean

Without the slightest notion
What you are supposed to do.
Are you the captain or the crew?

A stealthy corporate insurrection
Has reversed the ship's direction.
Those of us who left the shore

Twenty years ago and more
Bent over the brightly-coloured oars
Of the good ship Humanities

(So many oars on that ship were found
That it did nothing but go round and round
Elliptical, but it was fun)

Are now stranded on a steely fleet
Where everything is grey and sleek
And pointed at the bottom line

Which, for a ship, is most unwise.
Automatons in Star Trek suits
Advise on new research pursuits

In Scientology.
Slaves in the hold still groan and clank
As the voyage is sold to a different bank.

So we, the ancient mariners,
Are carefully covering things with tar
Small treasures and the things we love

So that though they smell of creosote
When we sink, they may float.

The Handdara of Ursula Le Guin
Invented in 1969
Worked strenuously to divide
Answerable from unanswerable questions.
Answerable ones they could even answer.
But these, they said, could never matter.
There are always more.
Nor will their answers cure
The urge to ask again.

Without discussing them at all
They preferred the unanswerable.
Years of a careful backward practice
Let them feel a question and *not ask it*.

Just so Wittgenstein's "mystical feeling."
I find it more and more appealing.
Wittgenstein also slaved and slaved
To work out what made sense to say
By proceeding negatively.
Endless fiddly propositions:
He made them up just to dismiss them.
So much for logical positivism.

Answers. Answers. Questions. Questions.
I for one am sick to death of them.

Twelve Angry Men is an old movie.
You'd think it had nothing more to say.
Committee work suggests to me
That the anger hasn't gone away.
There are angry women; there are angry natives;
White men are getting increasingly plaintive.
There are people of colour who are well pissed off.
We sit in small rooms and sniffle and cough through winter
    meetings.
Through tiny windows the sky is grey.
We sit and lie and lie and lie.
We gang up this way and we gang up that way,
Then consensually we declare our fatwa.

TED talks tell us that arts and science
Interpenetrate all the time.
Pop science tops bestseller lists.
Big data, environmental crit,
Science writing and rhetoric.
Cyborg critique and the Anthropocene.
Arts people know what scientists mean.
All of it boils down to this:
We'll never hire a scientist.

Computer scientists and engineers
Need to speak to their clients in ways that are clear
So they can make more money and better products.
So they turn to the arts and the onus is on us
To help them with their jobs.

Please do us this service.
Just not theoretically. That would unnerve us.
We do not need feminists. We dislike the word race.
Teach our students English, practically, case by case.
This is what we ask you, in simple good faith.

We don't know what you do and it's not important
To this request. Accept or ignore it.
If you can't give it, we'll seek it elsewhere
In commercial providers, board rooms and job fairs.
Most of your students are already there.

Let us be kind.
Your composition helps our bottom line.
So the deal is struck. And the arts mavens smile
Thinking of all the ways they'll beguile
Bemused engineers with critical theory

And the friends they will hire now they don't have to worry
About the job freeze. They will turn it around.
Communication entails profound
Critique of the system, of course, does it not?
We may be sold, but that's what they've bought.

Do we need another musical on literary theory?
Psychoanalysis makes us infinitely weary.
Everything it says about the brain has been disproven.
Neurophenomenology is where it's really moving.
Marx's hypothesis proved not to be descriptive;
The nation-state's still with us, and the only thing that's
    withered
Is our collective patience with a century of drivel.
Media's self-sustaining and does not require study;
Its engines are industry, warmongering and money –

This school needs to hire more women.
We're way behind in all the stats.
So much so that the time is coming
That we'll be punished by the government.
Here, my friends, is the answer to that.

There are women in Arts, apparently.
In English, say.
So, offer them a CRC – a precious Canada Research Chair.
The proviso is that it must apply to a woman they've already
    hired.
They'll change her title for free prestige
And we'll meet the metrics that we need.
Hire one woman twice, pay her once;
Cheap at the price. Equity.

Let's see what the professors say.
Oh. They agree. They have before.
There are principles and there's getting more.

Do nothing. Say nothing.
Buy nothing. Think twice.
I suppose it's okay to be nice.
For so many reasons
That's my advice.

Have you been upbraided by a chair?
It's like the man who wasn't there.
Speaking *ex officio*
The chair can talk down to you
While mostly being sat upon.
If we empower the furniture
God knows what they turn it to.

In composition, we must compose
All manner of things. The field is open.
Legal briefs and memos and notes,
Battlefield manuals for the drones.
Not much attention is paid to poems.

Philistinism begins at home.
It's really your fault your kids are dumb.
You are society.

Overworked, underpaid, angry, ignorant, afraid,
Here is another task for you:
Teach your kids before I do.

Mea maxima culpa
If I don't want to teach your daughter
The first facts she's ever seen
Or teach your illiterate son to read.

Please break their screens across your knees.
Nobody should reach eighteen
Knowing as little as they do.
And who's to blame? You.

No skills are soft. They're always hard.
Street school of smarts or Juilliard.
Skills are not you.

They're not your ego.
They're the things you're beaten into
In every martial arts movie.

Otherwise, just feel free
To be a no-skill bozo
Who in his own mind always thinks he'll

Be Adam or be Frankenstein,
Be Satan or be Oppenheimer
Just because he learned no grammar.

Considering that I'm an intellectual
I seem to concede they're ineffectual
A lot of the time.

Yet I do get mad
When dumbasses think smart people are sad.
When my daughter comes home
Ground down by the smart-girl jokes.
This happens less often to my son.
He's a bit of a spaz,
Which helps a lot
By making him look like something he's not.

Piss off, you cretins.
You can mock the answer if you get the question.
Please sign here to take the exam.
No? Can you explain –

Well, anyway.
It's inconsistent.
Like a covered woman can mock hijab
Or a Jew make Judaism an ass.
God help the rest.
Even in the wrong, we still know best.

I thought Myers-Briggs was a kind of aphasia.
Turns out that it's a test that can tell you
About your personality type
Without you having to live your life.

Type A's take it every year
To make sure it stays crystal clear
They're born to lead and not to cringe.
Upon their perfect answers hinge
A frail and anxious dominance.

B's do whatever it is B's do
Foggily and laissez-faire
Some answers here, some answers there.

Me, I leave all boxes blank
As a silent form of thanks
To my household gods for their divination.

A statistical numbers station
Calling out its mystic code
Tells me nothing I don't know.
I'm old.

I am a focus group of one.
Everything I focus on
Is tremendously important.
All the rest I just ignore.
That's what consciousness is for.

It is amazingly hard
To stay involved in the world at large
Considering the size of the planet
And the number of people on it.

Social media doesn't help at all.
It shows people up for what they are
In the aggregate.

Travel helps expend your wealth
But for making friends it doesn't help.
The folks you meet stay on the beach
Or in the hostel, earnestly.

Work is certainly important
But your workmates may be boring.

The news is perky and enthused
About horrors nobody would choose.

This is what religion's for –
Save for the fact it's total crap.
Adding a bunch of lies on top
Of human pain won't make it stop.

That leaves art in its myriad kinds:
The world as seen through other minds.

Did you know there are suffragette medals?
For survivors of the hunger strikes?
(I know this from *Call the Midwife*.)

They were not struck by the government.
(HM doesn't need to strike.)
So I guess they're not official.
Ask any veteran and I bet he'll
Grit his teeth and look polite.

Stars and stripes and scythes and crosses
Accommodate us to our losses.
Holloway was not Verdun.
Some medals are for those who won.

All behaviour at the gym is weird,
Aphasic, iterative. People sob and moan.
It looks like gospel. Women wear black pants
That emphasize their asses, regular as cassocks.

Ostensibly we're here for health
When we all know it's vanity.
In the sly and suffering eyes,
The furrowed brows and pumping thighs
We share this truth.

What has health ever done for you?
You had it for a while in youth.
It passed. You didn't miss it.
Wealth and power took its place
Fitter for the seated race
To which we're all committed.

Health buys you precious time, you say.
So does money, with less pain.
The spinners spin and the trainers train
The yoga bots do downward dog
To look better as days march on.

Let us be plain. To say that this
Relieves our stress is farcical.
The woman next to me, I think
Is actually strapped to her bicycle.

Cannabis exists to make up wellness deficits.
We're not doing this for health, only for the look of it.

Tuesdays, week after week
In the drugstore my daughter sees
A woman, morbidly obese, buying a stack of weight-loss
    magazines.
Not one or two. We're talking eight or ten.
She puts them on the counter, then
On top she puts a single chocolate bar.
It makes me sad, my daughter said.
The world is cruel, I said to her.

Sometimes it hurts when bias is confirmed.
Are you really gonna do that? Yes, you are.
Again, again, forevermore.

I've been dieting. Did you guess?
It's spring. I have Fear of the Dress.
It's wedding season. It's convocation.
It's whatever the fuck occasion.
So I'm starving and annoyed.
Retailers are overjoyed.

Women should be grateful for
Curvy jeans. BB Cream. The vote.

A few glass ceilings are showing cracks:
To many young women there's no pay gap.

We can cut our hair. We can go to work.
We can choose our own length of skirts.

Men can even wear them. It's solidarity.
Raise a cheer for gender parity.

We can do our manicures in the think tanks
And pay our mortgages to the big banks.

There are plenty of women on TV.
A woman named Bechdel is famous indeed.

Iceland has a woman prime minister.
Genital mutilation is known to be sinister.

Abortion is legal in civilized places.
If you say bad things people call you a racist.

At most intersections there is a stop sign.
Feminism has had its prime time.

YouTube influencers say it's all over
Untroubled by wars, laws, figures, or voters.

Women get peace prizes for surviving.
Never say women are not thriving.

Two twelve-year-old boys on the bus
Talking quietly, without fuss,
About Fortnite and other stuff.
Strikingly polite.
One of them mentions to the other
A book somebody recommended
About how to treat your friends, you know?
Bros Before Hos.
My heart goes cold.
The whole world is caught red-handed.
These two boys, how can they know
They've just described the *status quo*?
They just think it's good advice.

Two sobbing kindergarteners pass me by
It's mid-May and they still cry
All the way to school.
I'm waiting for the bus that will take me to the train
To the interview. I feel their pain.
They will struggle to nap on a mat on the floor
While I in a tiny room with a closed door
Will be faced with a mic.
Go away, mic! You are not my friend!
Eventually all my plosive p's will end
And I will skip out. As, I hope, will they.

Fish in the aquarium look neurotic.
They appear to be eternally circling clockwise.
Why is that?
Are they all right-handed, or do they prefer to lead with the
    right leg?
Is there a cultivated drift, blown in for order by the powers
    that be?
Or is it just what I prefer to see?
The downtrodden rays are desperately flat
And all their edges seem to be tattooed
Though they appear relaxed, if a bit subdued.
Other fish have been slammed in doors
Or pressed until they're paper thin
They flutter like parchment scraps an absentminded scholar
Happened vaguely to drop in.
Jellyfish appear on screens
Though they're the real thing.
Are they disturbed by elevator jazz and children's wails
Reverberating through the glass?
Clockwise through the world we pass.

Alterity. I don't believe in it.
I insist on making sense of fish.
Those ones there, floating vertically,
Are straight quotes in the text of sea.
Those ones, stitched neatly up the side.
And like all fish, expressionless,
Are obviously Frankenstein's monster fish.
And don't you wonder if
They find their tanks a bit too clean?
Have you seen the ocean recently?
This would explain their glassy eyes
And look of general reticence
Like poor people who've made the rent
And moved to rich suburbs.
Fish are not mysterious.
They are a lot like us.
Floating along, feeling guilty,
Looking sidelong for graffiti.

Benedict Cumberbatch is unperturbed.
He doesn't care about your inner life
But he isn't gay. He has a wife.
This drives people wild,
Especially English women
Who take coldness like communion.
Bless me by ignoring what I say.
By always looking the other way
Or flicking lint off your lapel.
Mushiness is gauche as hell.
Save it for the Gosling fans.
Isn't he Canadian?
He can shove his hey girl up his ass.
What we need is social class.
Eminently desirable, perfectly clear,
Propped up by height and Grecian hair
And a reasonable baritone.
Democracy is so unsexy.
God knows he saved us all at Bletchley.
Benedict, thy kingdom come.

It is obvious to all of us
That Russell Brand should be the next James Bond.
He's been working toward it his whole career.
Every coconut bra, every drunken leer
Has shown his facility for disguise.
We already know he can womanize.
I fail to see any other contenders
Who could do mouth-to-mouth on that franchise.
He might require some subtitling
In parts of the market, but all the frightening
Patricians are off being villains.
He should step in if he's willing.
Hoist the rag, take the king's shilling.
007 a little shorter, more manic and gleeful
Still perfectly good at killing people.

Simon Armitage is the new laureate.
He translated *Pearl*.
He did okay.
I'd never presume, but readers today
Can't understand that father's pain
As he once wrote it. Now it can be used
From the south to the north in therapy groups.
Especially in the midlands. Mr Pearl was their poet.
In London, wit was Chaucer's refuge
From the awful fact English wasn't cool.
Pearl isn't funny. Monty Python it's not.
It does not fear itself and gets on with the job.
Intricate, elegant, textured, secure,
Flawlessly present in its own despair.
A poem for grownups in a tongue half-grown
As Chaucer would tell you, if only he'd known
It existed. *Rum ram ruf:* he'd take it all back
And the BBC wouldn't sound like that.
I wish I could translate *Pearl*
But I'm not from that part of the world.

I recently remembered Rupert Brooke
In reading Byatt's *The Children's Book*.
What a bimbo.
His wittering brain full of Cambridge Plato
And sad refrains from Keats and Tennyson.
Poetry made to carve on walls
At terrible moments when language fails.
He could not know. He died too soon.
Colonial, not so warlike,
From an infected mosquito bite. Victorian.
Like dying from a shaving cut
Just before your execution.
In Tahiti he was not Gaugin.
Yet Brooke in his kinky boots
Saw the great Edwardian truth:
Better to die and get it over.
Embrace extinction like the dodo.
In that respect he was prescient.
The Tiresias of the Fabians
Which might have pleased him at the end.

O Douglas Adams, in your bliss
Tell us what the question is
To which the answer is 42.

That program will gamely run
Until the Natural History Unit's done
Filming its last unicorn.

Then, like Fermat's last theorem
It will slip by at a press conference.

The most racist things I ever say
Are when I am hanging up the phone
From an air duct cleaning call at home
At 7 p.m. as I'm cooking dinner.
We have no air ducts in the house.
The guy is calling from Bangladesh.
I make out half the words he says.
The whole thing is ridiculous.
We have no ducts! Take us off your list!
I say to this importunate South Asian.
I hang up without being rude.
It's not like it's a home invasion.
But I feel rage.

Now why is this?
We're both at opposite ends of a system
That makes us into mutual victims.
Few things are more horrible than cold-calling.
But what for me is so appalling
Is that I'm not getting what he says.
I'm in my house and totally failing to make him out.
It's giving me that flash of hate
Weirdly divided between me and him
And the situation we're in
Attenuated across the globe.

Why do we need machine learning
When there's an inexhaustible supply of people?
To give the programmers something to do,
As programmers are people, too?
The ones the government listens to?
How do I fit in to their data sets?
How do poets do in the aggregate?
More exactly, what
Do poets do in that domain?
How do they expect to account for it?
So far big data has yielded zip in the study of literature.
The numbers roll and the programs crunch;
People are more interesting over lunch.
Why should I admire Your Big Tool
When I desire nothing it can do?
Here in the Humanities
We are people talking civilly.
How can your machine trump me?

I said to my code jockey friend:
You're a white male technocrat.
There's nothing very subversive in that.
I know, he said, and grinned.
But I can pretend, and I still win.

There are scuttling pedestrians and assertive ones.
I do not feel assertive in front of two tons of metal and
    human error,
So I scuttle.
Yes, it's embarrassing. But I'm still alive.
My husband, assertive, has been hit three times.
Mind you, he's still living.
We always assume our behaviour is giving us an edge.
But does scuttling get me further ahead
Than the oblivious ear-budded tribes,
Who walk out in traffic and seemingly thrive?
Personally, I want them dead. At least, when I drive.

Or, when I am driven. I never grew up
And learned to drive. This explains a lot.

I live in a bicameral house.
On one side is the dining room
With a long table, a piano,
Most of the art and all the good dishes.
On the other is the kitchen and the TV,
Separated by a breakfast bar.
At any given time, half the family's there.
I was raised to think that TV while eating
Was the height of barbarity.
I peeked into the dining room today
And saw the Easter dishes not put away,
Washed and neatly stacked on the table.
There I stood in the front hall
Contemplating decline and fall.

It always gives you a jolt
To see your name on people you're not.
Surnames travel the world. They are found to belong
To all of the people we travel among.
Shtetl Jews named McPherson.
Black and white Bakers.
People named Ing either Asians or Quakers.
It freaks us out. Maybe in a good way.
But now that we've met them, what do we say?

We recently spent half a day without water.
A main was damaged outside my daughter's school
And took out the whole town.
That's 2000 teenagers unable to pee in her school alone.
We, still at home, at first were annoyed
That we didn't know why
Our taps wouldn't flow.
The city was slow in posting the news.
Social media blared self-importantly
But to little effect. No-one's twitter feed
Can stop ten million litres of flood.
But soon enough, after coffee and food
Important messages began to come through
From our colons. We could not flush.
My husband cycled off in a rush to a far-off café.
I took a bus.
What, I asked myself as I took a crap, will happen to us
When this is the norm? Very soon?
Everything is precarious.
Most of human culture
Has been conducted without running water
But we are not used to it.
We are not accustomed to shit in the moat
Or outside on the ground.
By the time we walked home the water was on,
Fitful and starting and exploding with air
From the pipes, which filled me with terror.
I was glad it was there.

An apothegm, in case you've not looked it up recently,
Is a short, pithy saying. A bit of general advice.
I've always liked them.
My son likes them, too. He calls them memes.
Pearls of dumb wisdom from communities
All over the place.
"We have seen the enemy and it is us!"
Is my all-time favourite, from Walt Kelly's *Pogo*.
Now wait just one minute, you say, I am peaceable –
I do my recycling. I never pick fights.
I have a decent horror of the alt right.
I have to ask – how that does apply to me?

If you exist, you're somebody's enemy.

The correct response to a book of riddles
Is to set it on fire.
Unless it's a manuscript of historical value
Proving that people were always assholes
Trying to be clever.
Aldhelm, I'd gladly shake his hand, provided
He spoke no riddles whatsoever
In English or Latin.
It's why you must always kill the dragon.
It's not the gold. It's the indirection.
You notice sphinxes are extinct.
Riddles are infuriating.
Elaborate metaphors are fine.
The parts are given. You put them together in your mind
To your own satisfaction.
A riddle is a dripping faucet or a ticking clock
You can't unplug and dare not destroy
Because you're saving it for the *Antiques Roadshow*.
For some folks they pass the time on long car rides.
I would rather be unconscious.
A riddle is just a hateful test
When most of us are doing our best.

I'd like to reassure you all
That among North American squirrels
The grey and black are the same species.
That's why they can interbreed.
Let that serve as a parable.

Some things become transparent as they age.
They get thin.
Tulip petals. Human skin.
Some become opaque.
Toenails or mussel shells.
Brains just sit there in the dark
So we can't tell.

Gnomics are rarely composed by gnomes
In their earthy homes, as described by Paracelsus.
Though it's fair to say that the earth is wise
In its salt and sulphur and mercury
And that all chemical formulae share a gnomic quality.

Herodotus was not low carb.
Hunting and gathering is improvident.
He gives a thousand useful rules for farms
And care of women, dogs and implements.

Don't take a horse on ice without rough shoes;
Trust no women whatever you do, says *Hávamál*.
Beware of trusting your son too soon.

There are childhood diseases
So the world is not overrun by babies,
The Exeter Book quietly intones.

He is wretched who lives alone.

A folly shared is not a folly halved.
Unfortunately, that is not the math.
While it may relieve your mind, it makes nobody smarter.
A folly shared is multiplied.
Thus when you apologize, no-one thanks you after.

More money is needed in the arts.
Skint people have swollen hearts,
Hot and pink with rage and need
Like the swollen bellies and knees
Of the poor in *National Geographic*.

People do not work for free.
Not in small presses, little magazines
And their slow churn of stories and poetry.
They work for love.
For mentorship, skills, acceptance, camaraderie,
Ego, lines on their CV. For the illusion of family.
They are so easy to abuse.

They will call out, these abused hearts
And kill the bodies of which they form the parts.
It all turns on a dime.
The dime they didn't get; the dime he said she said;
The dismal record of their wasted time.

Stand up comedy.
What about sit down comedy?
Lie in bed comedy, my personal favourite?
Fall over drunk comedy, admittedly hazardous?
Procedural comedy? Denotational comedy?
Etymological comedy?
I have nothing to say about ethnological comedy.
Computational comedy?
I have nothing to say about that either.
Plausibly deniable comedy?
Flat refusal of comedy?
Go away, comedy.

Yesterday at 11 a.m.
A little girl about four years old came out of her house
Across the street, staggering under the weight
Of a plastic play table – you know, one of those
Objects with flanges and dials and movable shit
That you distract your toddler with
At critical moments?
She bravely hauled it to the curb
And trotted away with bouncing curls.
I was floored. I thought of every toy and broken bit
Of crap we disappeared in the dead of night.
Consultation led to elegy.
It was up to us to throw old stuff away.
The nostalgia of the child is fierce and full of dread
Not the mild adult sentiment.
What went on inside that house
So that child could chuck it out?

Say I read that poem aloud.
Bemused parents in the room would exchange glances of
   sympathy
While non-parents loathed both them and me.
It's always a conspiracy.

Rodents gotta rode and readers gotta read,
Sowers gotta sow and breeders gotta breed.
These are our infinities.

These, and bleeders gotta bleed.

War, teeth, wheat, sex, poetry.
Knowers gotta know, seers gotta see;
Objectors object. Taxes gotta be.

Biology is old. It gets you in the neck.
For every new balance you have to write the cheque.
Everyone must eat and fuck
In the midst of scarcity and terrifying amplitude.

Giraffes are not polite. Neither are chinchillas rude.
Nonetheless they do a lot of what we do.
Mammals, animals, we share a habitat
Pole to pole, edge to edge, contiguous and tit for tat.

If you take more of this, there is less of that.

Pay what you owe.

What does this mean?

March dutifully with students as they protest climate change?
In plastic macintoshes underneath the corporate rain?
Take in more refugees?
Earth's been a migrant camp since before the Bronze Age.

Number-crunchers crunch and we're compelled to listen:
Everything that happens' the result of human vision.

The world in our minds is not the world outside.
A consumer doesn't think. A consumer only buys.
Thinking about consumption is not the act of shopping;
Talking about consumption is not the same as stopping.

We measure and atone. We estimate and pay.
We buy back such freedom as we have stochastically.
Guilt is sold by weight
Of compost and blood diamonds, things we love and hate,
In senseless increments, at variable rates.

Humans economize. We are born to trade.
Culture keeps producing. Nature wears away.

Hatred is a universal truth.
If you hate someone, assume that he hates you.
The weak hate the strong, the strong the weak.
Women men. Men women. Normals freaks.
Freaks normals. Even so
The silent despise those who speak.
Talkers hate those who sit silently.
Don't judge me, our teenagers say.
They judge each other constantly.
Judgement makes society.
I judge you wrong, I judge you right.
I do or do not like your tie.
Your head is covered and your head is bare.
For such judgements people die.
Hatred does not reside in any single group.
It surrounds everyone who isn't you like a heat haze.
You may even hate yourself – yet you persist.
You hate the government. You would not be missed
By them if you dropped dead. Or worse.
Every bond's sustained by its obverse.
There are too many people. Things are running out.
Yet we are rich in fear and pique and doubt,
Combustible as fossil fuel
And when we burn them, just as cruel.